ANIMAL SUPERPOWERS

DUNG BEETLES
Stronger than Ten Men!

Emma Carlson Berne

PowerKiDS
press

New York

Published in 2014 by The Rosen Publishing Group, Inc.
29 East 21st Street, New York, NY 10010

First Edition

Editor: Joanne Randolph
Book Design: Kate Vlachos

Photo Credits: Cover Kletr/Shutterstock.com; p. 5 Danita Delimont/Gallo Images/Getty Images; p. 6 E. R. Degginger/Photo Researchers/Getty Images; pp. 7 (sidebar), 14 Visuals Unlimited, Inc./Alex Wild/Visuals Unlimited/Getty Images; p. 7 James H. Robinson/Photo Researchers/Getty Images; p. 8 efendy/Shutterstock.com; p. 9 Heiti Paves/Shutterstock.com; p. 10 Johan Swanepoel/Shutterstock.com; p. 11 Peter Chadwick/Gallo Images/Getty Images; p. 13 James Hager/Robert Harding World Imagery/Getty Images; p. 15 Dorling Kindersley/Getty Images; p. 16 Juergen Ritterbach/Digital Vision/Getty Images; p. 17 Cosmin Manci/Shutterstock.com; p. 18 © Minden Pictures/SuperStock; p. 19 Marques/Shutterstock.com; p. 20 (sidebar) Alta Oosthuizen/Shutterstock.com; p. 21 Henrik Larsson/Shutterstock.com; p. 22 © iStockphoto.com/Casarsa.

Library of Congress Cataloging-in-Publication Data

Berne, Emma Carlson.
  Dung beetles : stronger than ten men! / by Emma Carlson Berne. — First edition.
      pages cm. — (Animal superpowers)
  Includes index.
  ISBN 978-1-4777-0748-7 (library binding) — ISBN 978-1-4777-0837-8 (pbk.) —
ISBN 978-1-4777-0838-5 (6-pack)
  1. Dung beetles—Juvenile literature. I. Title.
  QL596.S3B47 2014
  595.76'49—dc23
                              2012043256

Manufactured in the United States of America

CPSIA Compliance Information: Batch #S13PK6: For Further Information contact Rosen Publishing, New York, New York at 1-800-237-9932

Contents

Index

A
antibiotic, 13

B
babies, 4, 11, 13, 16–17, 20
burrow(s), 6, 11, 13

C
continent, 8

D
deer, 8
dung, 4, 6–11, 13–16, 20, 22

F
feces, 4

H
home, 4

I
insect(s), 4, 7, 22

L
larvae, 20

M
male(s), 13, 15, 18–19
manure, 4, 16, 22

P
parasites, 22
pile(s), 4, 6, 10, 14–16, 20
place, 4, 10, 22
pupae, 20

R
rollers, 10, 14

S
shells, 7
species, 6–7, 13

T
type, 4

Websites

Contents

Nature's House Cleaners

Have you ever visited a stable and seen piles of horse manure? You probably wrinkled your nose and stepped aside. Not all animals feel the same way you do. In fact, those manure piles are the home and food of the dung **beetle**. Without these six-legged superheroes, our world would be a messier place!

Dung beetles are a type of **insect** that collects animal **feces**, which is also called dung or manure. Dung beetles eat animal dung. They live in it and feed it to their babies. Dung beetles help keep our woods and pastures clean by consuming the waste other animals produce. In this book, we will learn more about these fascinating, useful beetles.

Some dung beetles roll the dung they find into balls, as this one has done.

5

So Many Beetles

There are more than 5,000 **species** of dung beetles. Some of the species are **nocturnal** and live in **burrows** beneath a pile of dung. Some species simply live in the dung. Other species are sometimes called tumblebugs. These beetles will build a ball of dung. The female beetle rides on the top while the male beetle rolls the ball along the ground.

This elephant dung beetle makes its home in Thailand. The people of Thailand actually eat some species of dung beetles!

These two scarab beetles have shiny, metallic shells. The outer shell of an insect is called its exoskeleton.

Some species of dung beetles are black, with shiny or dull shells. Others have beautiful multicolored **metallic** shells. All of these beetles must be very strong to move around the dung they collect. In fact, some beetles are stronger than ten full-grown men!

STRONGER THAN SUPERMAN

Like many insects, dung beetles are very strong. A species called *Onthophagus taurus* can pull 1,141 times its own body weight. That is the same as one human lifting 180,000 pounds (81,647 kg), which is the weight of six double-decker buses!

Almost anywhere on Earth that you find animals, you also find dung beetles. These strong, **industrious** creatures live on every continent except Antarctica.

They can live in the hot, humid tropics or the frigid tundra. They live in grassland, where they feed off the dung of cows, horses, elephants, and deer.

This dung beetle lives in a desert habitat. It uses its sense of smell to find and roll the dung of animals in the desert.

8

They live in forests, where they use the dung of foxes, raccoons, and rabbits. In the rain forest, they clean up the dung of monkeys and chimps. They can live in sandy soil or in soil that is mostly clay. Luckily for us, dung beetles can live in almost any environment. If they couldn't, the world would be full of a lot more animal dung!

This dung beetle lives in the forest.

Rock and Roll

Dung beetles have developed unique ways of moving the dung they depend on. **Rollers** mold the dung into balls and then roll it along the ground away from the dung pile. Sometimes, they simply eat the ball. Sometimes, though, a dung beetle looks for a good place to park the dung ball.

Often male rollers push the ball while the female dung beetle takes a ride on top.

Then it digs a trench or burrow underneath the ball so that it is buried a bit underground.

Now the ball is ready to be a nursery. The female dung beetle lays her eggs in the dung ball. When the babies are born, they will eat the dung.

Rollers use their strong legs to shape and move the dung ball.

1 One species of dung beetle, *Deltochilum gibbosum*, makes balls of all sorts of waste, not just dung. Chicken feathers and rotting animal flesh are just a couple favorites.

2 Some female dung beetles dig burrows that they fill with dung. The first male to arrive **mates** with the female and then guards the burrow entrance against all other males.

3 The ancient Egyptians believed dung beetles were related to the god of the rising Sun. They believed that this god rolled the Sun over the horizon, just as the beetles roll their balls.

4 Dung beetles have especially strong front legs, developed for molding and then moving the dung balls.

5 After dung beetles form the ball of dung, they climb on top and "dance." They are actually maneuvering the ball so that they can roll it in a straight line.

6 Dung beetle mothers produce a natural **antibiotic** in their glands. After they lay their eggs in the dung balls, the mothers apply the antibiotic to the balls to protect the babies from germs.

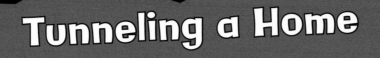

Tunneling a Home

Some dung beetles are called tunnelers or burrowers. Unlike the rollers, these beetles find a good pile of dung then dig a tunnel into and under the pile. Some of these tunnels can be almost 1 foot (30 cm) long. The tunnel ends in a room that the beetles have also dug.

Tunnelers use their strong legs to dig into a pile of dung rather than forming it into balls and rolling it.

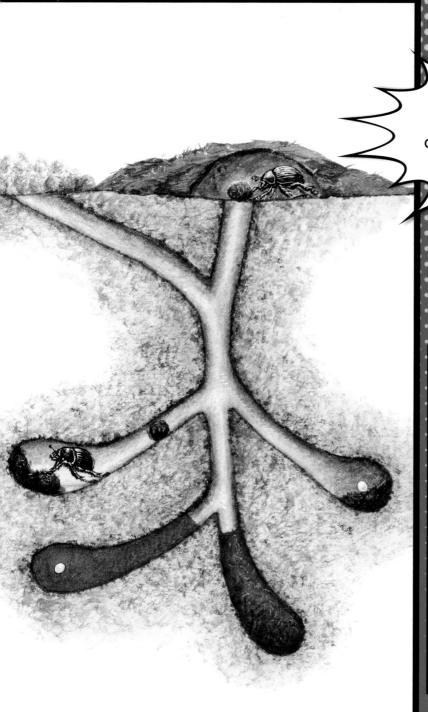

This drawing shows how a female dung beetle makes several tunnels under a dung pile. She then fills the ends of each tunnel with dung, where she lays her eggs.

Tunneler mates work together. The females do the digging. Then, the males collect pieces of dung from the pile. They both work to shape the dung pieces into balls. The female then lays her eggs in the small dung balls, which are placed in the rooms at the ends of the tunnels.

Dwelling Within

Unlike tunnelers, which dig through the dung pile and into the ground, dwellers dig into the dung and make their nests there. Many other beetles may make nests in the same pile of dung.

When the dung beetles called dwellers find a nice pile of manure, they just dig right into the pile. They build a room for their babies directly in the dung itself. The female beetle has a good system for doing this. She digs out the room and saves the pieces of dung from the digging. She then uses those pieces to make the ball in which she will lay her eggs.

When the babies are born, she stays in the nest with them. She makes repairs and also attacks any other beetles or beetle babies that may wander in.

This dung beetle, sometimes called the moose dung beetle, is one of the most common dwellers.

Ready, Set, Fight!

Rolling dung balls isn't the only reason dung beetles have to be so strong. The other reason is that they have to be ready to fight. Male dung beetles don't get to mate with just any female they choose. Instead, they use the strong "horns" on their heads and their powerful front legs to fight with other males.

These two dung beetles are fighting over a female.

Many male dung beetles, such as this rhinoceros beetle, have horns and spikes on their heads. They use them to fight and to attract mates.

The male that wins the fight then gets to mate with the female dung beetle. Sometimes, though, a male that lost a fight will wait quietly. Then he will sneak up on the female and mate with her when the winning male isn't looking.

Dung Beetle Babies

Dung beetles start their lives as eggs, deposited in dung balls by their mother. The eggs develop for about a week, then hatch into **larvae**, which are sometimes called grubs. These are the dung beetle "babies." The larvae eat the dung in the dung ball.

In about three weeks, the larvae become **pupae**. This means they become covered in a special coating and cannot move. Within this protective coating, the larvae change into adult dung beetles. When they are ready, they burst out of the coating. Then they walk or fly to another dung pile and begin to make their own dung balls.

GUIDED BY MOONLIGHT

Dung beetles are one of the only known creatures on Earth that use moonlight as a guide. The beetles can "measure" the angle of the moonlight. They then use that information to help them guide their dung balls in a straight line, away from the dung pile.

This is a dung beetle larva. It will eat the dung in which it rests until it is time to turn into a pupa.

21

It's a Dirty Job

Without dung beetles, the world would be a dirtier place. Animal dung can carry **parasites** and other germs that can make livestock sick. Farmers and ranchers need dung beetles to keep their pastures clean. Dung beetles clear away 80 percent of the cow manure in the whole state of Texas.

Dung beetles are hardworking insects. With their amazing strength, they keep our planet clean and make it a healthy place to live.

Dung beetles are helpful bugs. They clear away a lot of dung quickly. Thank you, dung beetles!

Glossary

antibiotic (an-tee-by-AH-tik) Matter that kills bacteria.

beetle (BEE-tel) A type of insect that has four wings and in which the outer pair are hard and protect the inner pair.

burrows (BUR-ohz) Holes animals dig in the ground for shelter.

feces (FEE-seez) The solid waste of animals.

industrious (in-DUS-tree-us) Hardworking or busy.

insect (IN-sekt) A small animal that often has six legs and wings.

larvae (LAHR-vee) Insects in the early life stage in which they have a wormlike form.

mates (MAYTS) Comes together to make babies.

metallic (meh-TA-lik) Something that looks similar to metal.

nocturnal (nok-TUR-nul) Active during the night.

parasites (PER-uh-syts) Living things that live in, on, or with other living things.

pupae (PYOO-pee) The second stage in the life of an insect that undergoes complete metamorphosis.

rollers (ROH-lerz) Dung beetles that roll dung into balls and then roll it away from the pile.

species (SPEE-sheez) One kind of living thing. All people are one species.

Index

A
antibiotic, 13

B
babies, 4, 11, 13,
    16–17, 20
burrow(s), 6, 11, 13

C
continent, 8

D
deer, 8
dung, 4, 6–11, 13–16,
    20, 22

F
feces, 4

H
home, 4

I
insect(s), 4, 7, 22

L
larvae, 20

M
male(s), 13, 15, 18–19
manure, 4, 16, 22

P
parasites, 22
pile(s), 4, 6, 10, 14–16, 20
place, 4, 10, 22
pupae, 20

R
rollers, 10, 14

S
shells, 7
species, 6–7, 13

T
type, 4

Websites

Due to the changing nature of Internet links, PowerKids Press has developed an online list of websites related to the subject of this book. This site is updated regularly. Please use this link to access the list:
www.powerkidslinks.com/asp/beetl/